T0387767

Animals Under Water

by Brenda McHale

Minneapolis, Minnesota

CREDITS

All images are courtesy of Shutterstock.com. With thanks to Getty Images, Thinkstock Photo, and iStockphoto. Front page - saulty72, Damsea. 1 - saulty72. 4&5 - Neel Adsul, wildestanimal, Ernie Hounshell, Jiang Zhongyan, Dan Kosmayer. 6&7 - frantisekhojdysz, Andaman. 8&9 - Steven L. Gordon, Vojce. 10&11 - Ewa Studio, photobeps, James Webb, Adam Ke, NatureDiver, tae208. 12&13 - Tory Kallman, Neirfy, chonlasub woravichan. 14&15 - Vladimir Wrangel, Yellow Cat, ND700. 16&17 - Sophon K, Eric Isselee, Vladimir Wrangel, Malgorzata Litkowska. 18&19 - Gerald Robert Fischer, Kristina Vackova, weera sreesam, leventalbas. 20&21 - Chase Dekker, Andrew Sutton. 22&23 - wildestanimal, dottedhippo. Background on all pages - Damsea.

Library of Congress Cataloging-in-Publication Data is available at www.loc.gov or upon request from the publisher.

ISBN: 979-8-88509-356-9 (hardcover)
ISBN: 979-8-88509-478-8 (paperback)
ISBN: 979-8-88509-593-8 (ebook)

© 2023 Booklife Publishing
This edition is published by arrangement with Booklife Publishing.

North American adaptations © 2023 Bearport Publishing Company. All rights reserved. No part of this publication may be reproduced in whole or in part, stored in any retrieval system, or transmitted in any form or by any means, electronic, mechanical, photocopying, recording, or otherwise, without written permission from the publisher.

For more information, write to Bearport Publishing, 5357 Penn Avenue South, Minneapolis, MN 55419.

CONTENTS

What Lives under Water? . . . 4
Wobbegong 6
Seahorse 8
Sea Star 10
Dolphin 12
Octopus 14
Jellyfish 16
Shrimp. 18
Blue Whale 20
Narwhal 22
Glossary 24
Index. 24

WHAT LIVES UNDER WATER?

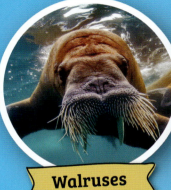
Walruses

Some of the strangest animals on Earth live under water. Which creatures can you find down there?

Sharks

Squid

Check out these fact files for a fast way to learn all about ocean animals. You'll explore each animal's **diet**, where it lives, and more.

SQUID

Type: Mollusk

Range: Oceans worldwide

Diet: Fish and crustaceans (kruh-STAY-shuhns)

WOBBEGONG

The wobbegong (WAH-buh-gahng) is a type of shark. It is sometimes called the carpet shark.

NAME Animals UNDER WATER | NO
NOM

WOBBEGONG

Type: Fish

Range: Pacific and Indian Oceans

Diet: Fish, octopuses, and crustaceans

This shark lies on the ocean floor like a shaggy rug. Creatures swimming nearby can't see the shark until it moves to eat them!

Some wobbegongs have tassels on their faces that look like beards.

A wobbegong's tassels and spotted skin help it hide by blending in with the ocean floor.

These sharks open their mouths wide to quickly suck in a tasty meal.

7

SEAHORSE

SEAHORSE

Type: Fish

Range: Warm coastal waters around the world

Diet: Plankton

Seahorses sometimes swim in pairs with their tails wrapped together.

These little creatures are always eating. Food goes through them quickly because they don't have stomachs!

For most animals, mothers carry the babies before they are born. But for seahorses, it is the fathers that carry the eggs.

A seahorse father can have more than 1,000 eggs at a time. But some babies don't live for long because the father eats them!

SEA STAR

Most sea stars have five arms, but some have many more!

SEA STAR

Type: Spiny-skinned creature

Range: Oceans worldwide

Diet: Clams, oysters, coral, and sponges

Sea stars have an eye at the end of each arm so they can see all around.

A sea star eats by pushing its stomach out of its mouth. The stomach wraps around food and then breaks it down.

A sea star has no brain, blood, or heart.

DOLPHIN

DOLPHIN

Type: Mammal

Range: Oceans worldwide

Diet: Fish, squid, and other sea creatures

Dolphins talk to one another with clicks and whistles.

Dolphins even have special sounds that they use as each other's names.

To make friends, dolphins stroke each other with their fins.

A blowhole

A dolphin pokes its head out of the water to breathe. It takes in air through a blowhole.

Dolphins sleep with one eye open so they can always watch for danger.

13

OCTOPUS

OCTOPUS

Type: Mollusk

Range: Oceans worldwide

Diet: Crustaceans and other mollusks

Octopuses can change color. This helps them hide or warn other octopuses of danger.

Octopuses push themselves forward by shooting water out of their bodies.

Some octopuses can use two arms to walk on the ocean floor.

Octopuses are very smart. Some can solve puzzles, open jars, and even copy other octopuses.

The suckers on an octopus's arms give the animal a strong grip.

If an octopus is in danger, it can spray ink at an attacker.

A sucker on an arm

15

JELLYFISH

Jellyfish eat and poop through the same hole.

A jellyfish does not have a heart or a brain.

JELLYFISH

Type: Boneless creature

Range: Oceans worldwide

Diet: Plants and small animals

Jellyfish disappear after they are washed up on the beach. They are made of mostly water and eventually dry up.

If you cut some jellyfish in half, the pieces will grow into two new jellyfish.

WARNING

DON'T TOUCH A JELLYFISH ON THE BEACH. IT MIGHT BE ONE THAT STINGS!

Box jellyfish are deadly. Just one could kill up to 60 people.

SHRIMP

There are thousands of different kinds of shrimp around the world.

SHRIMP

Type: Crustacean

Range: Worldwide

Diet: Plankton, plants, and small animals

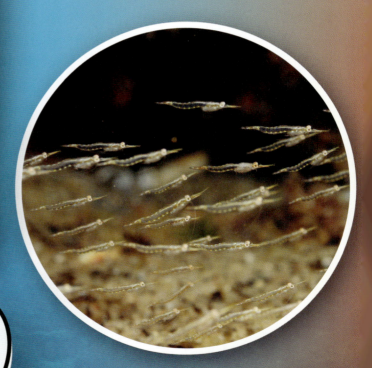

Shrimp live in rivers, lakes, and oceans.

The peacock mantis shrimp punches its **prey**. It has one of the fastest punches in the world for its size.

The pistol shrimp uses a large claw to quickly shoot a very hot bubble at its prey.

The Atlantic white shrimp can use its tail to jump out of the water.

BLUE WHALE

BLUE WHALE

Type: Mammal

Range: Oceans worldwide

Diet: Plankton

The blue whale is the world's largest living creature. It is bigger than anything that has ever lived, including dinosaurs.

A blue whale can be about as heavy as a house.

The blue whale's giant heart beats so loudly the sound can be heard from about 2 miles (3 km) away.

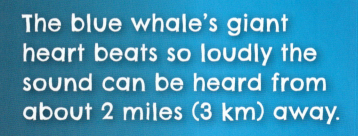

Blue whales call to one another with loud sounds. They are one of the loudest animals on Earth.

Like other whales, blue whales breathe through blowholes.

NARWHAL

A narwhal's horn is really a tooth called a tusk. It grows out through the animal's lip.

NARWHAL
Type: Mammal
Range: Arctic waters
Diet: Fish, mollusks, and crustaceans

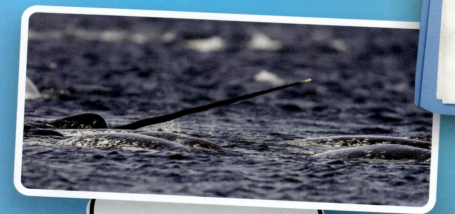

A narwhal's tusk can bend.

Most narwhals have one tusk. But some have two, and others have none.

These animals live in icy waters in the farthest north parts of the world.

Sometimes, two narwhals rub their tusks together to clean them.

Narwhals gather in groups of hundreds or even thousands.

GLOSSARY

Arctic related to the farthest north place on Earth

crustaceans animals that live in water and have hard outer shells

diet the kinds of food that a person or animal usually eats

mammal a warm-blooded animal that breathes air and drinks milk from its mother as a baby

mollusk a creature with a soft body, no backbone, and often a shell

plankton tiny animals and plants that float in oceans

prey an animal that is eaten by another animal for food

INDEX

blood 11
breathe 13, 21
eat 6, 8–9, 11, 16

eyes 10, 13
fish 5–6, 8, 22
mammals 12, 20, 22

mollusks 5, 14, 22
shrimp 18–19
sleep 13